Napkin Origami

Library of Congress Cataloging-in-Publication Data Available

10 9 8 7 6 5 4 3 2

Produced by Hollan Publishing, Inc.
100 Cummings Center, Suite 125G
Beverly, MA 01915
© 2008 by Hollan Publishing, Inc.

Published by Sterling Publishing Co., Inc.
387 Park Avenue South, New York, NY 10016

Distributed in Canada by Sterling Publishing
c/o Canadian Manda Group, 165 Dufferin Street
Toronto, Ontario, Canada M6K 3H6
Distributed in the United Kingdom by GMC Distribution Services
Castle Place, 166 High Street, Lewes, East Sussex, England BN7 1XU
Distributed in Australia by Capricorn Link (Australia) Pty. Ltd.
P.O. Box 704, Windsor, NSW 2756, Australia

Printed in China
All rights reserved

Sterling ISBN-13: 978-1-4027-5295-7
      ISBN-10: 1-4027-5295-4

For information about custom editions, special sales, premium and
corporate purchases, please contact Sterling Special Sales Department
at 800-805-5489 or specialsales@sterlingpublishing.com.

Photography by Allan Penn
Styling by Jennifer Dunlea

Cover and interior design by Carolynn DeCillo
Illustrations by Nick Robinson

The Pleated Wrap on page 102 was previously published in *Pliage des Serviettes* by Didier Boursin.

Napkin Origami

25 Creative and Fun Ideas for Napkin Folding

EDITED BY BRIAN SAWYER

STERLING/HOLLAN

An imprint of Sterling Publishing Co., Inc.

New York / London
www.sterlingpublishing.com

Contents

Introduction

Have you ever wanted to fold your table napkins into clever designs to impress your dinner guests and bring class and sophistication to your meals? Well, now you can, with this collection of beautiful origami creations in both cloth and paper.

While napkin origami has certain constraints that traditional paper origami does not, napkins—both cloth and paper—also afford greater forgiveness than standard paper in the folding and shaping sequences. Because most napkins aren't perfectly square, you will need to use a certain skill and judgment to bring about the desired results. For the more formal pieces, applying spray starch is a vital prerequisite, and once a cotton napkin is dried and ironed, the crisp material becomes remarkably malleable, yielding strong, restaurant-worthy creases and curves.

If this is your first venture into origami, you'll want to start by learning the basics of folding (see pages 2–7) before attempting to complete your first model. Since many of the designs in this book require you to pleat the material to create a concertina, or fan, appearance, pay particular attention to the mathematical-division procedure, although a more random, freestyle method is usually acceptable.

Home stores sell both paper and fabric napkins in a variety of colors and patterns. Take care to begin with the material facing in the correct direction (up or down), as most napkins are colored or patterned on only one side. If the napkin is the same color on both sides, fold two different colored napkins together as one to create a two-toned effect, if one is desired. Always fold on a clean, flat surface, such as a dining table. If you have lots of napkins to fold for a large banquet, fold them well in advance of the meal so the shape and rigidity become set.

Be creative with props to decorate or accompany the completed projects. Adding toys to the carousel or rocket ship brings a nice personal touch to a child's birthday party setting, while flowers or gifts can add romance to the more formal designs.

And now, enjoy turning your meals into exciting occasions with your napkin creations!

Signs and Symbols, Tips and Techniques

The instructions for each project in this book include tips and techniques relevant to creating that particular design. But before you begin your first project, you should also familiarize yourself with the following signs and symbols, which derive from the internationally recognized visual language used within standard origami. Knowing these techniques and terminology will assist you in understanding how to fold in general, as well as help you in interpreting the directions for fashioning a particular piece.

Symbols

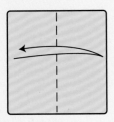

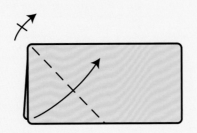

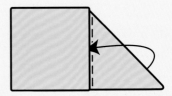

Fold and unfold.

Repeat the step behind/on the reverse side.

Tuck part of the flap inside

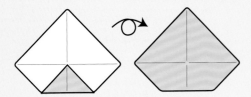

Turn the napkin over.

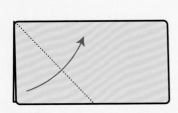

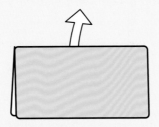

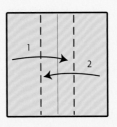

X-ray vision (shows the hidden view).

Open out/unfold.

Do step 1 before step 2.

Fold dot to dot (shows exactly where to make a certain fold).

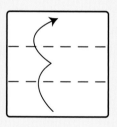

Fold over, and over again.

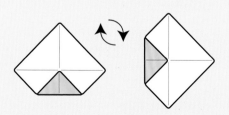

Rotate the napkin to a new position.

Pleat the napkin.

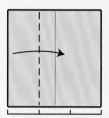

Divide the napkin into thirds or another specific fraction.

Push in or flatten a certain portion of the material.

Valley-fold directional arrow.

See the following sections for explanations of valley folds and mountain folds.

Mountain-fold directional arrow.

Valley Fold

A *valley fold* is made in a forward direction, with the folded portion remaining in view. Always try to fold the material away from you, from the bottom to the top, as shown. The projects in this book that utilize a valley fold reiterate this. A valley-fold crease is indicated by a line of dashes and the directional arrow shown in the Symbols section.

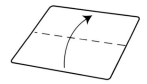

Mountain Fold

The reverse of a valley fold, a *mountain fold* is made in a backward direction, moving a certain part of the material behind and out of sight. Such a crease is indicated by a line of dashes and dots and the directional arrow shown in the Symbols section.

This procedure needs to be done carefully, especially when using delicate fabrics. The directional arrow is open-headed, usually disappearing behind the edge of the material.

Waterbomb or Pyramid Base

The *waterbomb base*, also known as a *pyramid base*, is used as the foundation for projects such as the rocket ship (page 32) and the carousel (page 96).

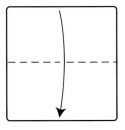

1. With the napkin completely opened out and the colored or patterned side down, fold the napkin in half from the top to the bottom.

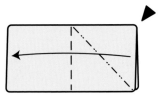

2. Grasp the lower right-hand corner (single layer only) and carefully drag it across to the bottom left-hand corner.

Prefolded paper napkins already have the vertical center crease required for the motion accomplished in step 2. For fabric napkins, first precrease the napkin on the dotted line.

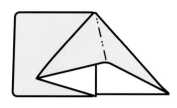

3. Step 2 in progress.

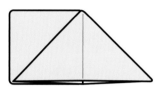

4. Step 2 completed. Carefully turn the napkin over.

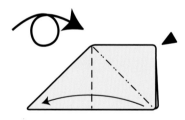

5. Repeat step 2 on the side now facing you.

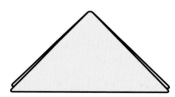

6. The completed waterbomb base.

Inside Reverse Fold

The following steps illustrate the origami technique of *inside reverse folding*. To practice the technique, use a small rectangle of paper, folded in half lengthwise.

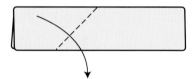

1. Make a random valley fold on a sloping crease across the paper. Crease the paper well.

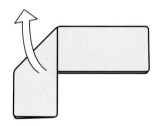

2. Open out the step 1 fold.

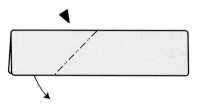

3. Opening out the principal fold from below, push down the near end of the spine crease so that it inverts between the two layers; in other words, push this section inside, between the two layers.

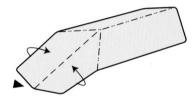

4. Step 3 in progress. The near end is valley-folded in half, while the remaining paper is once again flattened.

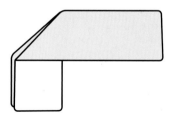

5. The completed inside reverse fold. Compare this fold with the outside reverse fold, described next.

Outside Reverse Fold

The following steps illustrate how to achieve an *outside reverse fold*. To practice the technique, again use a small rectangle of paper, folded in half lengthwise.

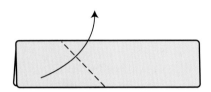

1. This time, fold the two open edges upward, making a sharp valley crease at a random desired angle.

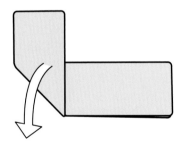

2. Open out the step 1 fold.

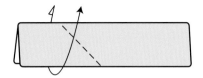

3. Opening out the principal fold, this time push down along the near end of the spine crease and turn the two main layers outside on themselves.

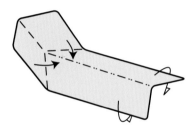

4. Step 3 in progress. Collapsing the far end of the material on a mountain fold, flatten the two layers at the near end together.

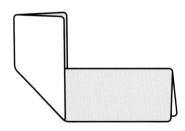

5. Step 4 completed. Compare the result with the inside reverse fold, described in the previous section.

Pleating into Sixteenths

This technique is a mathematical method for creating the perfectly even pleats required for several of the projects in this book. It creates a series of horizontal creases that can later be refolded into rows of pleats. To practice the technique, take a square of paper and arrange it as a diamond, as shown in step 1.

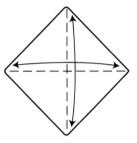

1. Fold the paper in half diagonally both ways, folding and unfolding each time.

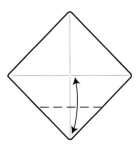

2. Fold and unfold the upper and the lower corners to where the diagonals cross (the center of the paper).

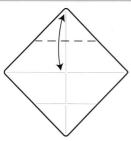

3. Step 2 completed. You have now divided the paper into quarters horizontally.

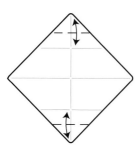

4. Halve each outermost section by folding and unfolding the upper and the lower corners to where the creases made in step 2 cross the vertical diagonal crease.

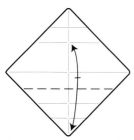

5. Halve each inner section by again folding and unfolding the outer corners, this time bringing each corner to where the crease made in step 2 nearest the other corner crosses the vertical diagnaol crease.

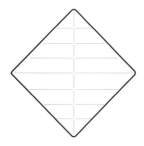

6. Step 5 completed. You have now divided the paper into eighths horizontally.

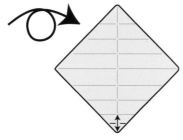

7. Turn the paper over. Now, to divide the paper into sixteenths, make valley creases on this side of the paper between the one-eighth creases. Begin by folding and unfolding the upper and the lower corners to where the closest creases to them intersect with the vertical diagonal crease.

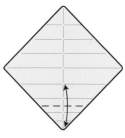

8. Continue folding and unfolding, each time skipping two creases in, and placing the horizontal valley fold precisely and logically in between existing one-eighth creases. At the end, you will have divided the paper into sixteenths horizontally.

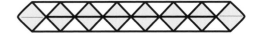

9. By collapsing the paper back and forth toward the center using the creases made in steps 2 through 8, you will have a pleated, or *concertina*, effect end to end.

Use this technique for such projects as the leaf (page 14) and angel's wings (page 110), and when creating your own formal designs.

Simple Models

This opening section presents designs that require only a few simple folds.

Pirate Ship

TRADITIONAL

With the theme of Halloween or pirate play in
mind, use a large black fabric napkin of a heavy,
textured variety. The initial stages of this procedure
are very simple, but you will need to practice
turning the lower edge outward on itself in steps 5
and 6 to create the hull of the ship.

Pirate Ship

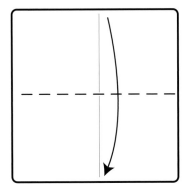

1. With the napkin completely opened out and the colored or patterned side down, fold the upper edge of the napkin down to the lower edge.

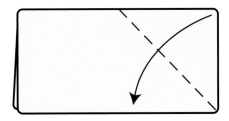

2. Fold the upper right corner down at a 45° angle.

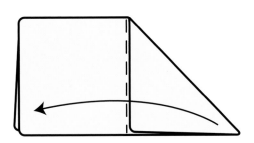

3. Fold the lower right corner across to the left.

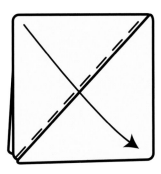

4. Wrap the upper right corner down over the other layers.

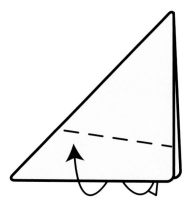

5. With your fingers centrally placed between the lower layers of material, begin turning the opening at the bottom outward on itself.

This rolling motion is meant to be deeper at the front of the hull.

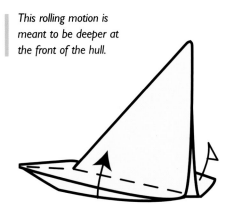

6. Step 5 in progress.

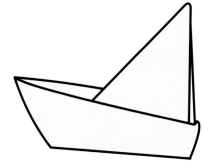

7. The completed pirate ship.

Leaf

GAY MERRILL GROSS

It doesn't matter how many pleats you make in the opening steps of this procedure, or whether you use a paper or a fabric napkin; this simple design adds a touch of elegance to picnic and other alfresco dining.

Leaf

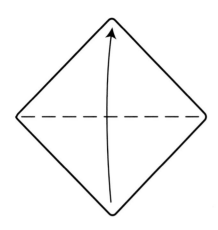

1. With the napkin completely opened out and the colored or patterned side down, fold the napkin diagonally in half from the bottom to the top.

3. Step 2 completed. Mountain-fold the lower end underneath.

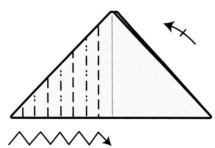

2. Divide each side, left and right, into a series of vertical pleats, creating a concertina effect (see page 6). Do not fold the vertical centerline; leave this open as you gather the two lines of pleats inward.

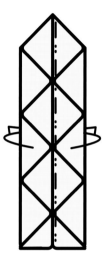

4. Mountain-fold the napkin in half vertically along the center crease, pinching the lower layers together tightly and allowing the pleats to fan open.

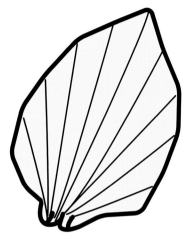

5. To shape the leaf, manually stretch the pleats open further while also curving the napkin into a soft convex form.

Fish

NICK ROBINSON

Use a marble, olive, seashell, piece of sea glass, or anything that's the right size to suggest an eye in this attractive creation, which is ideal for a seafood dish. A starched heavy fabric napkin is recommended.

Fish

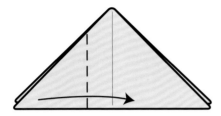

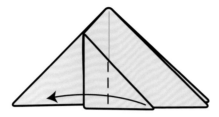

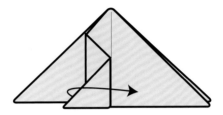

1. With the napkin completely opened out and the colored or patterned side down, make a waterbomb or pyramid base (see page 4). Fold the left corner, single layer only, to the midpoint of the right half of the triangle.

2. Fold the flap back along the vertical crease at the center of the triangle.

3. Swing the flap back to its position before step 2.

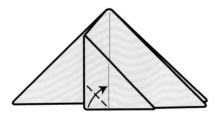

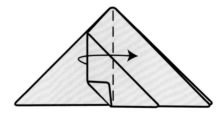

4. Fold the small lower-left corner of the flap to line up with the vertical center.

5. Fold the entire upper section of the flap from left to right, across the vertical center.

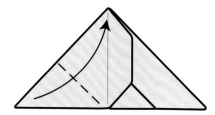

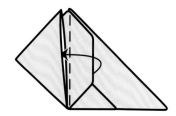

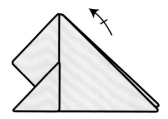

6. Fold the lower-left corner of the main triangle to touch the upper corner.

7. Open the pocket of the flap created in step 6, and carefully tuck the flap on the right into the pocket. Allow the triangular flap at the bottom to swing over. This will become the fish's tail fin.

8. The left side is complete. Repeat all steps on the right side.

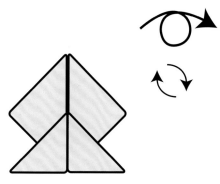

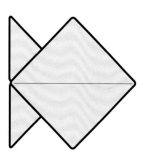

9. Both sides are complete. Turn the napkin over and rotate.

10. The completed fish. Add the eye as shown in the photograph.

Shirt and Tie

TRADITIONAL

Perfect for a Father's Day dinner, this crisp, formal design deploys both a starched cloth napkin for the shirt and a paper napkin for the tie. To create a tie in a reasonable proportion to the shirt, use a paper napkin a quarter of the size of the cloth napkin. Ideally, use a white napkin for the shirt.

Shirt

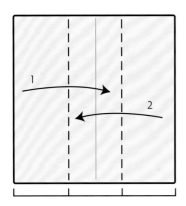

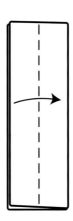

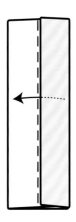

1. With the napkin starched and completely opened out, fold the napkin vertically into thirds, folding the left side first and then overlapping with the right side.

2. Fold the left raw edge (single layer only) back on itself to align with the folded edge on the right side.

3. Repeat step 2 with the hidden edge, making the napkin symmetrical.

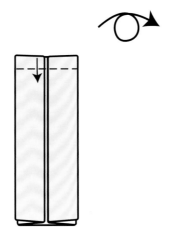

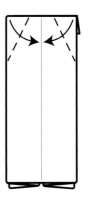

The corners finish up along the vertical centerline, but the angles of the folds are quite sharp.

4. Fold the upper edge down by about 1 inch (2 centimeters). Turn the napkin over.

5. Fold the two upper corners down.

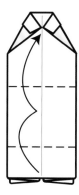

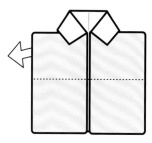

6. You have now formed the collar of the shirt. Double the lower edge of the shirt over twice, with the first fold about half as deep as the second fold. Tuck the resulting folded edge under the collar flaps.

7. The body of the shirt completed.

8. If you wish, you can now suggest sleeves on the shirt by carefully sliding out a single layer of the folds made in step 6 on each side of the body of the shirt (shown here by X-ray dots).

9. Adjust the sleeves, noting that the shoulders of the shirt assume a deeper angle the more the sleeves are pulled out.

Tie

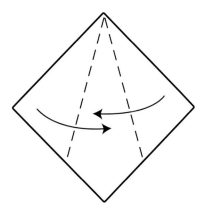

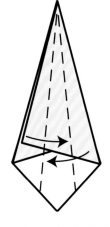

1. With the paper napkin completely opened out and the colored or patterned side down, arrange the napkin as a diamond. Then, fold the two sides inward, with one flap overlapping the other.

2. Narrow the napkin by folding it into thirds once more.

3. Fold the top corner across on an angled crease. The distance depends on how long you want the completed tie to be.

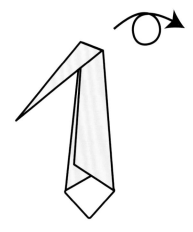

4. Step 3 completed. Turn the napkin over.

5. Fold the excess paper at the point back across to the left, opening the inside folds a bit as necessary to create a kind of knot.

6. Mountain-fold the remaining paper of the upper point behind the tie and tuck it in between the layers. This completes the knot.

7. Tighten and arrange the knot to complete the tie. Place the tie on top of the shirt, with the knot tucked underneath the flaps of the collar, as shown in the photograph.

Emperor's Robe

GAY MERRILL GROSS

Perfect for a Japanese meal, this elegant design, accompanied by beautiful chopsticks, doubles as a stylish utensil holder. Use fabric with an Asian pattern for this piece.

Emperor's Robe

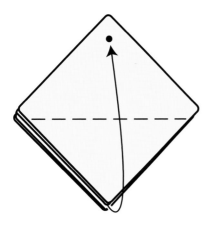

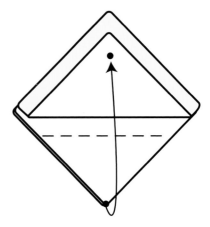

1. With the napkin completely opened out and the colored or patterned side down, fold the napkin into quarters and arrange it as a diamond, the open edges all at the bottom. Fold the first layer up to a point just below the top corner.

2. Fold the second layer up to a point just below the top corner of the first folded layer.

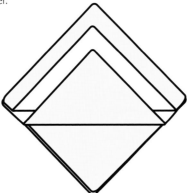

3. Step 2 completed.

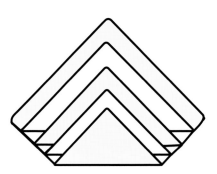

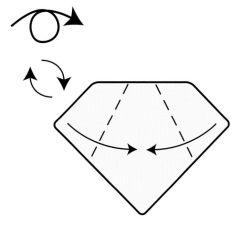

4. Repeat step 2 with the remaining two layers.

5. Carefully turn the napkin over, rotate 180° and fold the two sides inward at an angle, allowing them to overlap across the chest of the robe.

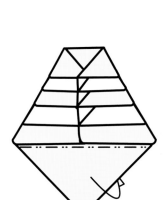

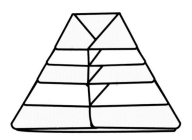

6. Mountain-fold the excess material behind the robe.

7. The completed emperor's robe.

Rocket Ship

LARRY HART

This fantasy creation, ideal for a child's birthday party, should be fashioned from a silver paper napkin. Use a yellow plate to suggest the moon, or place the napkin directly on a black placemat or tablecloth, representing the night sky. Finish by scattering a few assorted stars around.

Rocket Ship

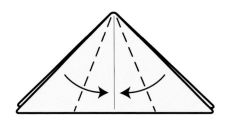

1. With the napkin completely opened out and the colored or patterned side down, make a waterbomb or pyramid base (see page 4). Fold the sloping edges (single layer only) down to the vertical centerline.

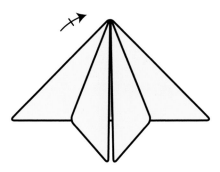

2. Step 1 completed. Turn the napkin over and repeat step 1 on the new side.

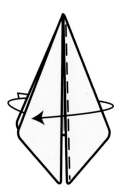

3. Like you were turning the page of a book, fold the right half of the model (top layer only) over and across to the left side, using the vertical center crease. Repeat this step behind, with the underside left layer.

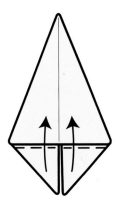

4. Fold both lower corners (single layer only) up over the central horizontal edge.

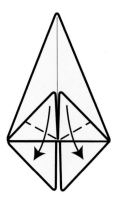

5. Fold the points back down again on an angled crease, creating the legs of the rocket.

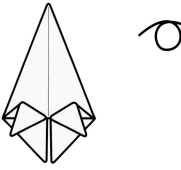

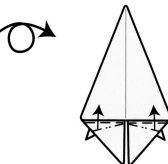

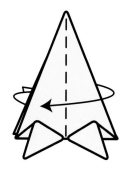

6. Step 5 completed.

7. Carefully turn the napkin over and repeat steps 4 and 5 on the new side.

8. Repeating step 3, fold the right half of the model (top layer only) over and across to the left, using the vertical center crease. Repeat this step behind, with the underside right layer.

A small triangular squash fold automatically forms at the upper end of each leg as this move is completed.

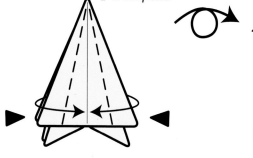

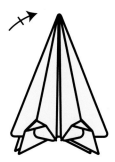

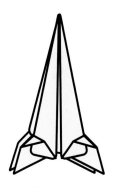

9. Narrow the body of the rocket by folding the outer sloping sides inward to the center crease (single layer only, left and right).

10. Carefully turn the napkin over and repeat step 9 on the new side.

11. The completed rocket ship.

Ice Cream Cone

RICK BEECH

This design cleverly uses two napkins (paper or fabric) overlaid and slightly offset to produce a whimsical result. The lower napkin should be light brown in color, for the cone. The upper napkin can be whatever "flavor" you wish.

Ice Cream Cone

For the plate-sized model shown in the photograph, use paper napkins prefolded into quarters. Use completely opened-out paper or fabric napkins for a "giant" cone and scoop.

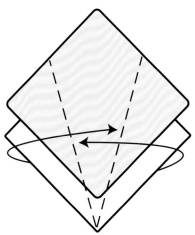

1. With the "flavor" napkin on top of the brown napkin and the colored sides of both facing down, fold the napkins as one into thirds, trisecting the bottom angle.

2. Step 1 completed.

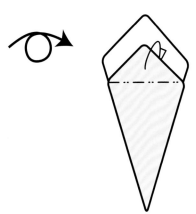

3. Carefully turn the napkins over and square off the top of the cone by mountain-folding the corner behind it and tucking it inside.

4. Make a narrow pleat horizontally across the cone to give it a more realistic shape. The upper crease is a mountain fold, the lower a valley fold.

5. Pinch the upper corner into a soft *crimp* to give a round form to the ice cream.

6. The completed ice cream cone.

Whirligig

LOES SCHAKEL-SANDIFORT

Based upon the Japanese origami technique of *purse* folding, this elegant creation requires a 4-ply paper napkin with a fairly strong weave. Some precreasing is involved, so be patient and make all the folds carefully and accurately.

Whirligig

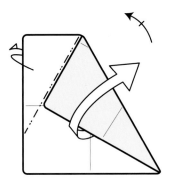 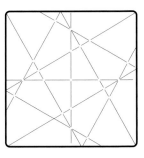 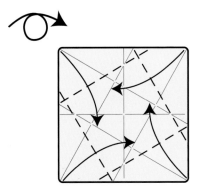

1. With the napkin completely opened out and the colored or patterned side down, fold and unfold the napkin in half both vertically and horizontally to mark the vertical and horizontal centerlines (most conventional paper napkins already have these). Fold the upper right corner across to meet the horizontal crease line, with the fold beginning at the lower right corner.

2. Using the edge of the flap folded in step 1 as a guide, mountain-fold the excess material at the upper left corner behind the napkin. Crease the napkin well. Unfold the napkin and repeat steps 1 and 2 with the remaining three corners.

3. The completed crease pattern thus far. Turn the napkin over.

Whether you work around clockwise or counter-clockwise, you will need to adjust the arrangement of the layers when you reach the last flap; hence, you should take care that everything is symmetrical, with each flap overlapping its neighbor.

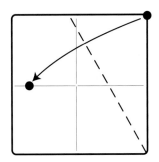 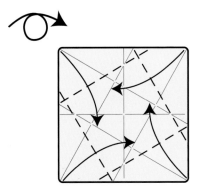 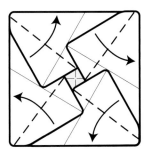

4. Refold all four corners inward on the creases made in step 2.

5. Step 4 completed. Peel back each of the inner flaps so it lays along the outer folded edge.

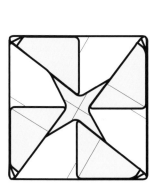

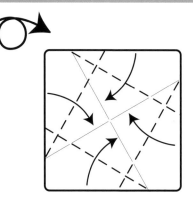

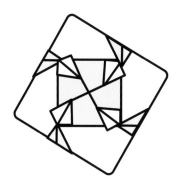

6. Step 5 completed. Turn the napkin over again.

7. Repeating step 4 and using the creases made in step 1, bring all the corners inward, again overlapping them symmetrically. This step is like closing a cardboard box without tape: each flap is slipped partially under its neighbor.

8. Step 7 completed. Turn the napkin over once more.

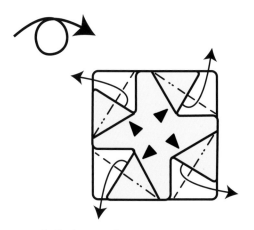

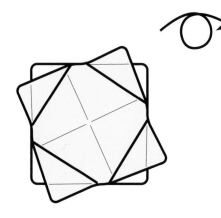

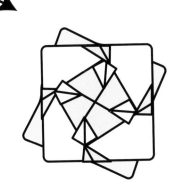

9. Placing one finger under the raw edges of the four small pockets created by the previous folds, pull the paper outward to the side, squash-folding the excess material into the position shown in step 10.

10. Step 9 completed. Turn the napkin over once more.

11. The completed whirligig.

Heart

FRANCIS OW

Use either a paper or a cloth napkin for this design, which is perfect for Valentine's Day or any romantic meal.

Designs for Special Occasions

This next selection of designs, created especially
for holidays and special events, includes more complex
techniques for shaping the final design.

Santa

GAY MERRILL GROSS

This Christmas party design uses three paper napkins, two red and one white, all the same size. As an optional flourish, you can add small spherical sweets for the eyes and buttons (not shown in the photograph).

Santa

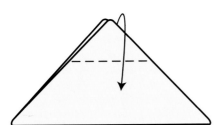

1. With the first red napkin completely opened out and the colored side down, fold the napkin in half diagonally. Fold the top corner (single layer only) down by one third.

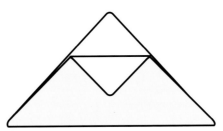

2. Step 1 completed.

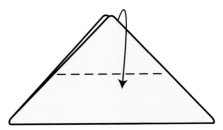

3. Completely open out the white napkin and then fold it in half diagonally. This time, however, fold both layers of the top corner down, bringing the tip a little below the base edge.

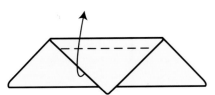

4. Fold both layers back up again, creating a pleat approximately 1 inch (2 to 3 centimeters) wide.

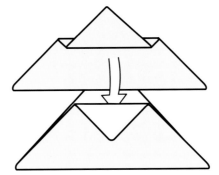

5. Slide the white napkin down between the two layers of the red napkin until the two folded edges align.

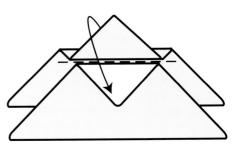

6. Fold the upper section down, creating a white beard.

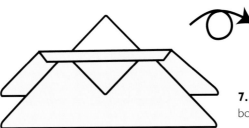

7. Step 6 completed. Carefully turn both napkins over as one.

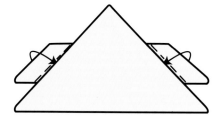

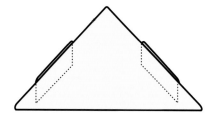

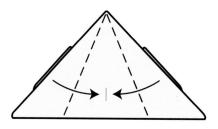

8. Fold the excess tabs inward over the edge of the central red triangle and tuck them behind the upper layer.

9. Step 8 completed. The X-ray lines show the position of the excess material.

10. Fold the two sloping edges inward to the vertical centerline.

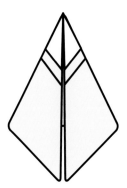

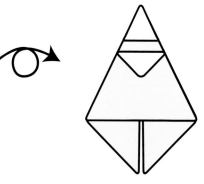

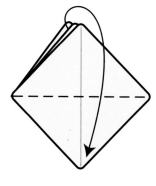

11. Step 10 completed. Turn the napkin over.

12. Step 11 completed.

13. Fold the other red napkin into quarters. Then, fold it diagonally in half, from the top to the bottom.

14. Lay this triangle underneath the body to create arms. The X-ray dots show the correct position of this napkin.

Baby Bootee

NICK ROBINSON

Perfect for a christening party, this design uses a
paper napkin in either white, pink, or blue. You can,
of course, make a pair of bootees for each setting!

Baby Bootee

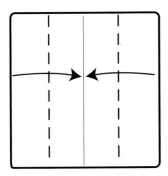 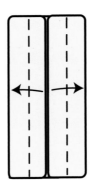 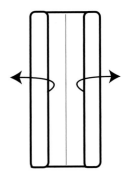

1. To achieve the baby-sized bootee shown in the final photograph, begin with the napkin prefolded into quarters and treat all four layers as one. Fold the left and right sides to the center.

2. Fold the edges at the center back out to the folded edges.

3. Fold out the double layers on either side.

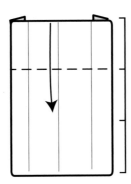 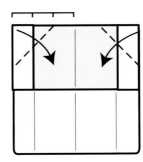

4. Valley-fold a crease about one third of the way to the top.

5. Fold both top corners down to about two thirds of the way from the top.

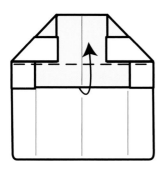 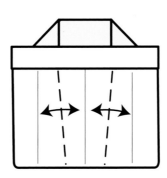 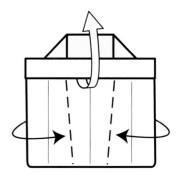

6. Fold a single layer upward to trap the two triangular flaps.

7. Make two creases that slope slightly inward to the lower center point.

8. Lift and open the top of the model, folding in and overlapping the lower flaps.

9. Fold a small section of the lower edge behind.

10. The completed bootee. Carefully put a finger inside, open the lower section a little and round the heel.

Rose

TRADITIONAL

A thin-ply paper napkin is ideal for this design,
perfect for Valentine's Day or any romantic meal.

Rose

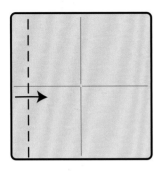

1. Begin with a napkin printed on both sides with the same solid color. With the napkin completely opened out, fold a vertical border of about 2 inches (5 centimeters) along the left edge.

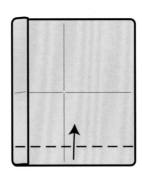

2. Fold a similar border along the lower edge.

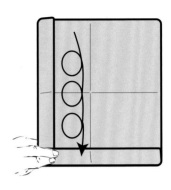

3. Place the index and middle fingers of your left hand on top of the lower left corner, gripping the material with your thumb underneath. Pull the upper section of the napkin down over your fingers to begin creating a cylinder.

4. Continue pulling the napkin around and around until you have a roll extending from your fingers.

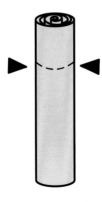

5. Arrange the roll vertically. About 2 inches (5 centimeters) down from the top (the edge between your fingers), pinch it in and collapse the sides. Everything above this pinch is the bud.

6. From the pinch downward, twist the material to make the stem. You can twist it quite firmly; the paper will not tear. Twist until you are about halfway down the length of the roll from the initial pinched paper.

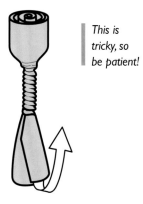

This is tricky, so be patient!

7. Lift the outer raw corner (the end of the roll) up and begin carefully teasing it away from the roll. Everything will lift as one piece initially; separate layers and use the forgiving nature of the material to raise a "puffed-up" point, while leaving the roll pretty much as it was.

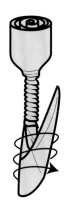

8. Scrunch up the lower section, and beginning where the leaf joins the stem, twist downward to complete the stem.

9. Step 8 and the form of the rose completed.

10. To finish, look down at the bud from above. The flower head appears rather hollow and lacking in petals. Create the illusion of a much fuller bloom by taking hold of the inside corner and continuing to twist it carefully in the direction it is already going. This tightens the inner spiral and draws in the layers.

11. Beginning on the outside and working inward, turn over the upper edge of the bud so that from the side, the petals appear separated and staggered. This gives the completed flower a more authentic appearance.

Bunny

RICK BEECH

This quirky design uses a heavily starched white napkin and can be shaped to taste at the conclusion. Rearrange the ears, reposition the head, and adjust the angle of the tail—whatever suits your fancy.

Bunny

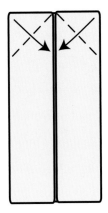

1. With the napkin completely opened out, fold the two outer vertical edges to the center, then fold the upper corners downward at 45° angles.

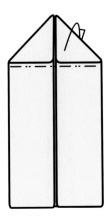

2. Mountain-fold the upper corner behind the napkin.

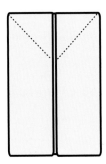

3. Step 2 completed. The X-ray lines show the new positions of the flaps formed in step 1.

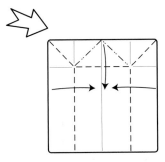

4. Unfold everything. Collapse the napkin on the existing creases. The upper edge comes toward you, then the two sides refold to the vertical centerline.

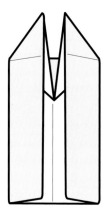

5. Step 4 in progress.

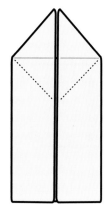

6. Step 4 completed. The X-ray lines show the positions of the hidden layers.

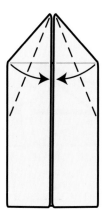

7. Fold the corners in to the vertical centerline.

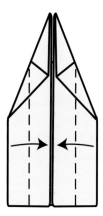

8. Fold the two outer edges in toward the vertical centerline.

Party Hat

DAVID NEALE

To make this cheerful design, use a 4-ply paper napkin with a bright pattern, preferably on both sides of the material. Work carefully, pressing all the vital creases into place (gentle ironing at the end also helps), and take special note of how the layers are arranged during the folding sequence.

Fun napkins with a pattern or color on both sides can be hard to find. If you can't find any you like, but are ambitious and intent on achieving just the right look, you can glue two napkins together, back to back, as was done for the model in the photograph.

Party Hat

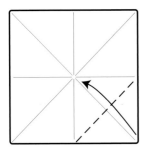

1. With the napkin completely opened out and the colored or patterned side down, locate the diagonal creases as well as the vertical and horizontal lines by folding and unfolding the napkin horizontally, vertically, and in both diagonal directions. Fold the lower right corner to the center.

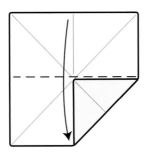

2. Fold the upper edge of the napkin down to the bottom.

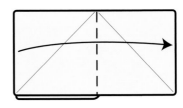

3. Fold the napkin in half from the left to the right.

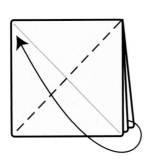

4. At the lower right corner, fold *two* layers across the paper diagonally, then rotate the napkin so this new corner is at the top.

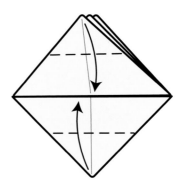

5. Working with one layer at a time, fold each layer to the center, upward and downward.

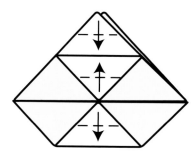

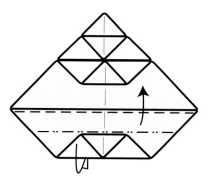

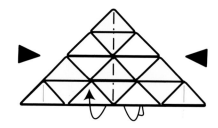

6. Halve the upper section with a simple valley fold, repeating throughout.

7. Make a final pleat in the lower section, first folding the material up on the valley fold (the lower edge of the finished hat) and then down again on the mountain fold.

8. Press everything flat (gently iron if you wish). Open out the front and rear layers of the hat from beneath and pull them apart. The corners of the hat will push in toward each other, and you can flatten the entire napkin, forming a diamond shape.

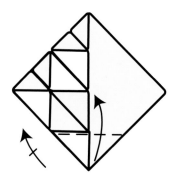

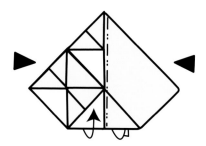

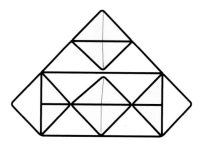

9. Fold the lower corner up. Repeat this step on the other side of the hat.

10. In almost a reversal of step 8, open the napkin out along the two lower edges, pulling the edges in opposite directions, and then flatten the material, returning it to its shape in step 8.

11. The completed party hat.

Innovative Creations

The designs in this section use additional props in the final presentation. Some can be supported or modified by flatware at the table, while others are designed to hold flatware, food, toys, or even other napkins.

Peacock

TRADITIONAL

How deliciously clever to fold a regular sheet of paper into the body of the creature and then to use fancy paper napkins to make the spreading tail! The sheet of paper should be about 6 inches (15 centimeters) square (a paisley or marbled pattern in blue or green works well), and the two napkins should be delicate paper napkins of a standard size.

Peacock

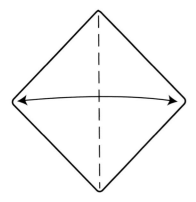

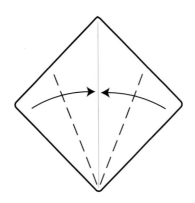

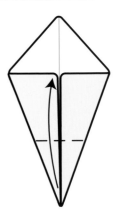

1. With the sheet of paper positioned with the colored or patterned side down, fold and unfold the paper in half diagonally to establish the vertical center crease.

2. Fold the lower adjacent edges to the centerline to form a kite shape.

3. Fold the lower point up to the edges of the two flaps folded in step 2.

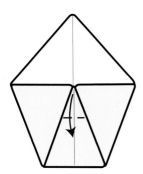

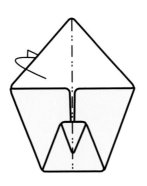

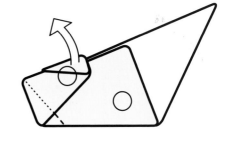

4. Fold this point downward a small amount.

5. Mountain-fold the model in half along the vertical center crease. Rotate the paper as shown.

6. Holding the bird by the lower edge (indicated by the circle), grasp the head section between the finger and thumb of your other hand. Swing the head upward and forward, flattening the paper and making a new crease (indicated by the dotted line).

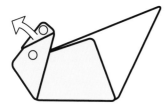

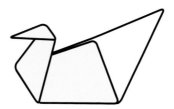

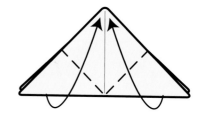

7. Again hold the neck where shown and lift up the beak, flattening it into position.

8. The completed body.

9. With the two napkins completely opened out and the patterned side down, fold each napkin separately into a waterbomb or pyramid base (see page 4). Fold the sharp points (both layers) to the upper corner.

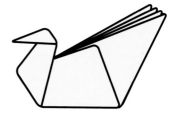

10. Carefully mountain-fold each of the napkins in half.

11. Slide one of the napkins inside the body, just beneath the outer layer (the wing), and push it far inside to ensure the tension of the paper and the earlier folds hold the tail feathers in place.

12. Repeat step 11 on the reverse side with the other napkin to complete the peacock.

Swan

EDWIN CORRIE

This design uses a heavyweight paper napkin. Often termed *luxury napkins*, these napkins feel almost like felt and come in several earthy colors. Fold this piece of traditional origami very carefully, and make sharp creases throughout.

Swan

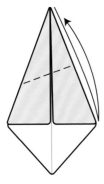

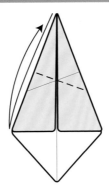

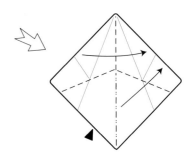

1. With the napkin opened completely and the colored or patterned side down, fold the napkin to step 3 of the peacock (page 76) and rotate it 180°. Fold the upper corner to the lower right corner, crease, and unfold.

2. Repeat the fold in step 1, this time taking the upper corner to the lower left corner. Crease and unfold.

3. Unfold the napkin completely. Now comes a rather challenging collapse of the paper, but the necessary creases are all in place. Holding the lower corner, make a valley fold on the right side (continuing the downward crease that starts at the center), turning the vertical crease into a mountain fold as you do so. The lower corner swings across to the right. At the same time, fold the upper left side over to the right using the valley creases. The paper collapses to the right, with a pointed corner sticking out from between the two layers. See the illustration in step 4 for guidance.

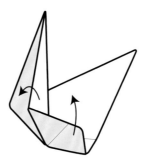

5. Step 4 in progress. You can see how two operations happen simultaneously.

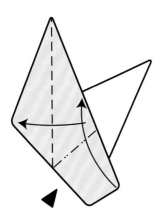

4. Step 3 completed. On the existing crease, fold the raw edge forward to sit along the front edge of what will become the swan's neck. At the same time, swivel the lower flaps up.

6. Step 4 completed. Repeat step 4 on the reverse side.

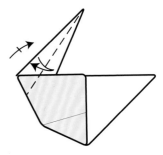

7. Fold and unfold the front outer layer of paper along the edge of the neck. Repeat on the reverse side.

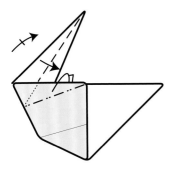

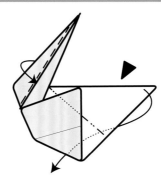

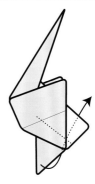

8. Refold step 7, but as you do so, swivel the excess paper behind and inside, running the mountain-fold crease carefully to the point of the wing. Repeat on the reverse side.

9. Fold the front edge of the neck back to the right and tuck it inside the pocket formed by the previous steps. Make an inside reverse fold with the tail flap, noting that the crease begins just behind the neck.

10. Inside-reverse-fold the tail point back out again. The dotted line shows the new position.

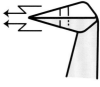

13. The head in progress. Make two narrow, parallel inside reverse folds to create the beak.

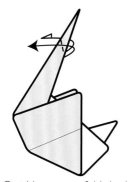

11. Outside-reverse-fold the head.

12. Pull the layers of paper out from within the underside of the head to make it wider. Shape the back of the body by mountain-folding the edges inside. This will help the final model stand better.

Because the model in the photograph was made using a sufficiently heavy paper napkin, it stands on its own without support.

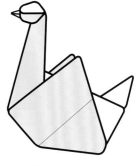

14. If desired, slide the body of the swan between the prongs of an upturned fork, which will help keep the model upright and together.

Butterfly

J.P. WYSEUR

Ideal for summer barbecues and alfresco dining,
this fun design uses a brightly colored napkin,
either paper or fabric.

Butterfly

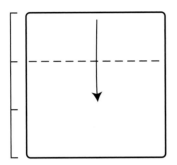

1. With the napkin completely opened out and the colored or patterned side down, fold the upper edge of the napkin downward by one third.

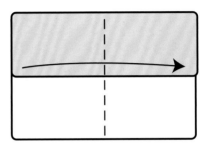

2. Fold the napkin in half from the left to the right.

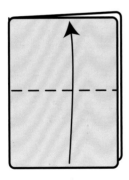

3. Fold the napkin in half from the bottom to the top.

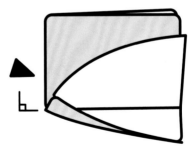

4. Open the principal front flap (two layers) out so it stands at a right angle to the rest of the material, and squash-fold the corner.

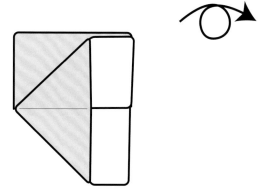

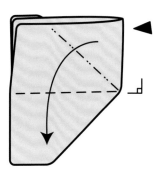

5. Step 4 in progress. Note that a triangle forms as the upright layers open flat. Turn the napkin over sideways.

6. Repeat step 4, but on the reverse side.

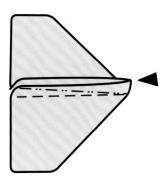

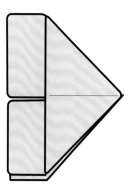

7. Step 6 in progress.

8. Step 6 completed.

Butterfly

These creases do not meet the outer corners, but land just short.

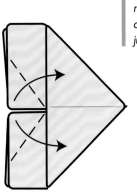

9. Fold the inner corners on the left side outward on the creases shown.

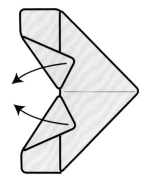

10. Unfold step 9.

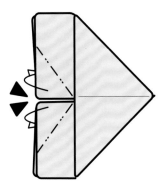

11. Inside-reverse-fold the flaps folded in step 6 inside the model.

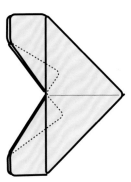

12. Step 11 completed. The X-ray dots show the positions of the inside reverse folds.

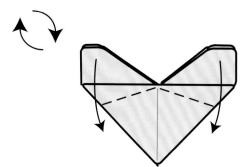

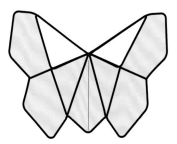

13. Rotate the model 90° so the flaps from the wings are now at the top. Fold the upper wings (single layer only) downward on each side to create the lower wings. The angle you use should suit your own personal taste.

14. Step 13 completed. Notice the loose triangular flap at the inner part of each lower wing. For a color change, and to neaten the model, tuck these flaps inside the principal layer of each lower wing.

The body shaping (step 15) and use of a fork (step 16) work well only with paper napkins because of their reduced size and thickness. The model shown in the photograph is fashioned from a thick fabric napkin.

15. To make the body more realistic, pinch in a narrow ridge down the center of the napkin. The central crease becomes a mountain fold and the two other creases become valley folds. A small upside-down V shape will form along the creature's body.

16. The completed butterfly. If desired, slide the body of the butterfly onto the central prong of an upturned fork.

Dessert Server

TRADITIONAL

This napkin design doubles as a holder for the vital utensils for the sweet course! Use a heavyweight paper, or luxury, napkin (see page 78).

Dessert Server

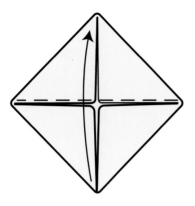

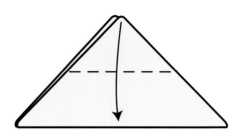

1. With the napkin completely opened out and the colored or patterned side down, fold all four corners of the napkin to the center. Fold the lower corner to the upper corner.

2. Fold the upper corner down to the lower edge.

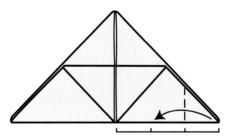

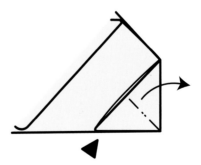

3. On the right side, fold the sharp point inward one third of the distance to the center.

4. Open out the upper layers of this point and squash-fold it into a diamond shape.

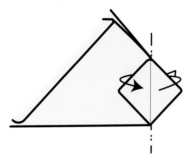

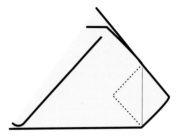

5. Using the natural hinge crease of the diamond, carefully swivel the outer half of the napkin behind while folding the inner half across to the right. The diamond disappears underneath.

6. Step 5 completed. The X-ray lines show the position of the small diamond section.

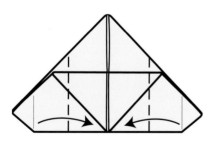

7. Repeat steps 3 through 6 on the left side. Fold both outer vertical edges toward the center, making sure that the two diamonds slightly overlap. Flatten all the creases.

8. Place the utensils inside the pocket created by the horizontal fold made in step 2 to complete the dessert server.

Bread Holder

TRADITIONAL

This design, which looks marvelous in either paper or fabric, can hold bread, rolls, or perhaps pieces of fruit.

Bread Holder

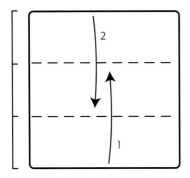

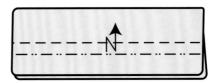

1. With the napkin completely opened out and the colored or patterned side down, fold the napkin horizontally into thirds, beginning with the bottom and following with the top.

2. Make a vertical pleat in the upper layer only. The valley-fold crease runs centrally down the middle, and the mountain-fold crease runs below, one sixth of the total height, forming a centralized column.

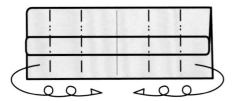

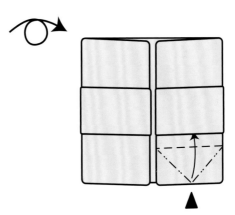

3. Step 2 completed. Mountain-fold the napkin vertically into thirds, doubling the two shortest ends over twice to make a compact bundle. The new folded edges should meet at about the middle. Turn the napkin over.

4. Step 3 completed. Fold an outer edge (single layer only) inward, squash-folding all the corners into diamond shapes. Tuck these diamond shapes beneath the central pleat.

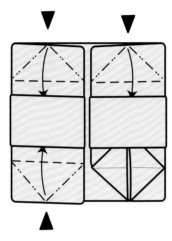

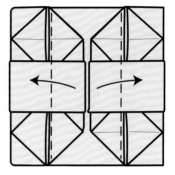

5. Repeat step 4 on the three remaining corners.

6. Press all the folds flat, then open out the two panels to sandwich the bread in between, as shown in the photograph.

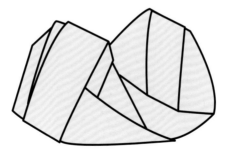

7. The completed bread holder.

Carousel

TRADITIONAL

This design not only gives your kids something to do at the dinner table, it also serves as a fun way to introduce them to table etiquette. Use a starched fabric napkin in a bright color or pattern, and adorn the spokes of the carousel with small toys, as shown in the photograph.

Designs for Formal Dining

Using starched pure white or solid-colored napkins
and a sophisticated design can add a wonderful
elegance to any formal meal.

Pleated Wrap

DIDIER BOURSIN

Fashion this design from a starched white cotton napkin and use it to decorate a wine bottle.

Pleated Wrap

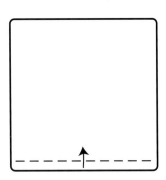

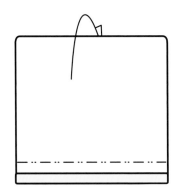

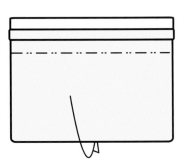

1. With the napkin completely opened out and the colored or pattered side down, fold up a narrow horizontal border along the lower edge. This border should be approximately one sixteenth the height of the napkin.

2. Mountain-fold the upper section behind, creating a border twice as wide again as the first one. You now have two horizontal strips at the top edge.

3. Step 2 completed. Mountain-fold the lower section behind, similar to what you did in step 2, leaving a slender border of similar width.

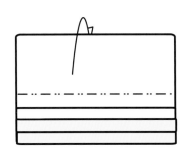

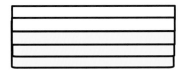

4. Again, mountain-fold the upper section behind, allowing another border of a similar width to show from the front.

5. Repeat step 3 (folding motion not illustrated here). You should now have five horizontal stripes facing you.

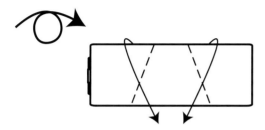

6. Carefully turn the whole napkin over. Fold the upper corners down at the angle shown in step 7.

7. Carefully interweave the pleats from each side of the napkin beginning with the second pleat from the bottom.

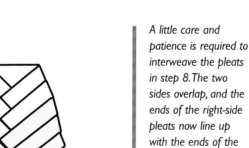

8. Step 7 completed.

A little care and patience is required to interweave the pleats in step 8. The two sides overlap, and the ends of the right-side pleats now line up with the ends of the left-side pleats.

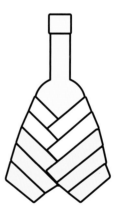

9. Slide the napkin over the neck of a wine bottle and allow the napkin to rest on the bottle's shoulder. The pleats may slide apart slightly, depending on the size and shape of the bottle.

Fountain

TRADITIONAL

This exceptionally elegant design is created using a simple starched cotton napkin, the kind favored by restaurants. The lower section is placed inside a narrow glass, such as a champagne flute, while the two upper ends of the pleated material cascade over the sides.

Fountain

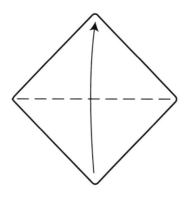

1. With the napkin completely opened out, fold it in half diagonally.

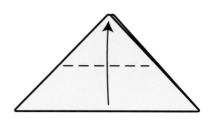

2. Fold the napkin in half from the bottom to the top.

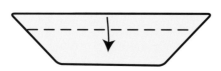

3. Fold the upper edge (single layer only) back down one third of the way toward you.

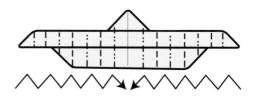

4. Step 3 completed. Concertina pleat (see page 6) the entire napkin, bringing each of the ends in toward the center.

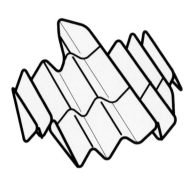

5. Step 4 in progress.

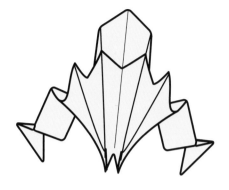

6. Hold the lower section tightly together while allowing the upper section to fan open.

7. Place the napkin in a narrow, shallow glass for the final presentation.

Angel's Wings

TRADITIONAL

Many fabric designs require heavy starching and ironing to create a stunning table piece, but the effort is certainly well worth it for this design. Use a pure white cotton napkin, the kind found in high-end restaurants.

Angel's Wings

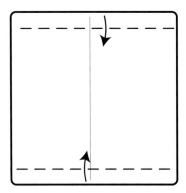

1. With the napkin completely opened out, fold a narrow border horizontally along both the upper and the lower edges. These borders should be approximately 1 inch (2 to 3 centimeters) deep.

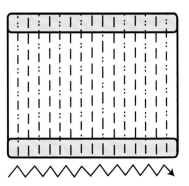

2. Vertically pleat the napkin into sixteenths, beginning at the left side with a mountain fold and working your way evenly across the material to the right side (see page 6).

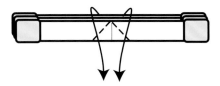

3. The borders folded in step 1 lay on the top side of the fabric. Fold down both ends of the long strip of pleats to sit along the centerline, as shown.

4. Step 3 completed.

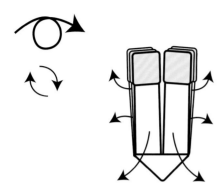

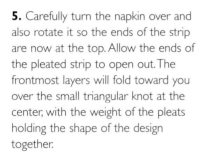

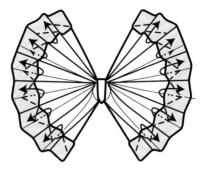

5. Carefully turn the napkin over and also rotate it so the ends of the strip are now at the top. Allow the ends of the pleated strip to open out. The frontmost layers will fold toward you over the small triangular knot at the center, with the weight of the pleats holding the shape of the design together.

6. With the raw edges of the two borders folded in step 1, create a small V-shaped tuck in between each of the pleats. Do this by lifting the edge of the material up while compressing the pleated layers together.

7. The completed angel's wings.

Nautilus Shell

JUN MAEKAWA

Use a fairly coarse-textured fabric for this simple yet incredibly striking design. Luxury cocktail napkins create a perfectly sized display for formal drinks and hors d'oeuvres.

Nautilus Shell

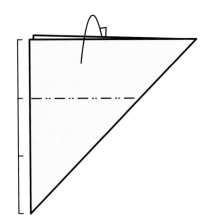

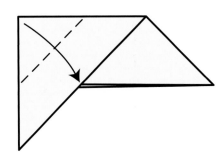

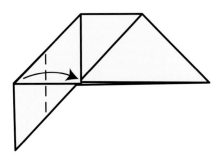

1. With the napkin completely opened out and the colored or patterned side down, fold the napkin in half diagonally. With the folded edge running diagonally, mountain-fold the upper third of the material behind the napkin.

2. Fold the upper left corner down at a 45° angle. The corner section should be a square.

3. Fold the left vertical edge inward, halving this extra material.

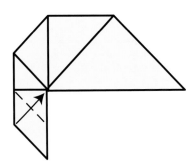

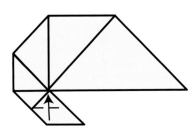

4. Make another 45°-angle fold. You should see the beginning of a spiral effect.

5. Repeat step 3.

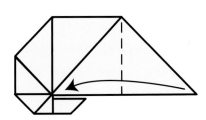

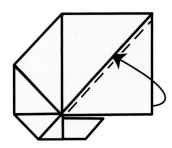

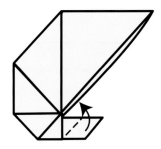

6. Fold the right corner to the center of the model.

7. Fold the lower triangular flap into the pocket above it.

8. Fold the small flap over, as in step 4.

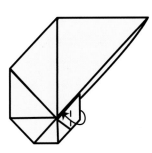

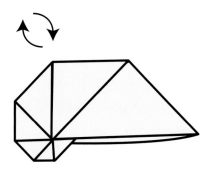

9. Fold the same section inward again, tucking it inside the model.

10. Rotate the napkin to the position shown and round the opening slightly for the completed nautilus shell.

Rosette

PAUL JACKSON

This charming design, ideal for both formal and romantic dining, can be folded from either a paper or a cloth napkin.

Rosette

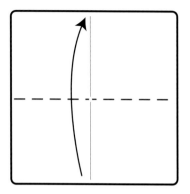

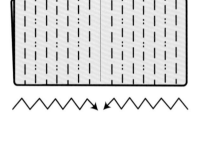

1. With the napkin completely opened out and the colored or patterned side down, fold the napkin in half from the bottom to the top.

2. Vertically pleat the napkin into sixteenths (see page 6). Leaving the two central columns as they are, concertina-fold all the other sections toward the center.

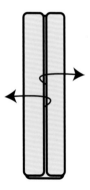

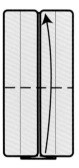

3. Open out one layer on both the left and the right side.

4. Carefully fold the napkin in half from the bottom to the top.

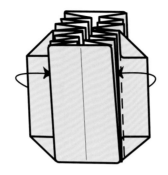

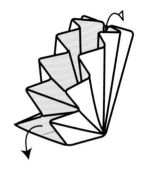

5. To join the two halves of the rosette, first fold over all four outer corners at 45° angles.

At the top, fold both layers as one.

6. Further secure each side by doubling over the left and right protruding sections and tucking each between the first set of neighboring pleats.

7. Step 6 completed. Carefully open out the rosette, separating the front and rear layers.

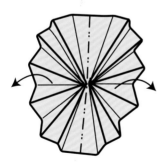

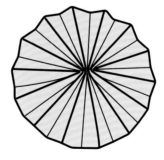

8. Allow the pleats to spread apart. Allow the central spine to "snap" into place as the entire model takes the appearance of a full circle.

9. The completed rosette.

Index